JLGERHARDT

Godscout

.COM

WANT TO SEE GODY LOCK

LIVE OR DIE

How to lose everything, make yourself nothing,
and rejoice through anything

a study
in Philippians | JL Gerhardt

I am tired of living little.

Tired of measuring meaning in likes and shares, identity in colored jerseys and brand names, purpose in paychecks and happiness in latte foam.

I am tired of believing popularity and safety and comfort matter. Tired of holding so tightly, fists clenched, closed around things I can touch but can't feel, things with no gravity and so much pull.

I am tired of trying to belong in the dark. Tired of this wilderness people call paradise with its cold shadows and crushing waves and cocktails that never quench your thirst.

I am tired of living little, every day on this never docking cruise ship a charade. I am sick of stillness and conformity, of making a goal of not rocking the boat.

I am ready to tip it over.

I am ready to wake up to an apocalypse. I am ready for the ground to shift and the sky to split open. I am ready for the world as we know it to end so that something next, something unknown, something big can break through.

I am ready to step through the mirror, to partner with the unseen forces of light and love led by the suffering Savior, Captain, King, to lay down my life and take up HIS cross, to abandon the glitter and the hype and the me-centered days for a forever of living as HIS grateful, glorified slave.

I am ready to live. I am ready to die. Live or die, I'm in.

Table of Contents

How To Use This Study •—

This study is intended to accompany the book of Philippians, encouraging and empowering personal and/or collective study of God's Word. Read it one session at a time, working through all the questions and prayer prompts before moving on. If you're studying alone, work at your own pace. If you're studying with a group, consider covering and discussing one session per week. The essays between study sessions are intended to prompt meditation and reflection.

As we proceed, know: this study won't be an exhaustive look at the book of Philippians. Instead, we'll read a few verses each session, ask some helpful questions, consider the context, pray, and meditate on some reorienting truth— all in an effort to connect us to God and get us living more sold out lives.

Oh—and don't skip the Introduction! It's where you'll want to start, and I'm confident it will bless you as you enter into this study.

INTRODUCTION

Welcome to the book of Philippians! Grace and peace to you from God our Father and the Lord Jesus Christ! This ancient book has been challenging and shaping Christians for generations. It's a call to surrender. A call to contentment, courage and trust. A call to lose everything you have and gain everything that matters. If you're anything like me, that's an exciting (and slightly terrifying) proposition.

Philippians is a letter written by the apostle Paul, likely in prison in Rome, to the church in Philippi, a "leading city" in Macedonia (modern day northern Greece). Look, I drew you a map. Don't laugh.

Philippi was situated at the foot of a mountain, beside a marsh and adjacent to the Aegean Sea. Then, Philippi was known for its proximity to gold mines and well protected by city walls erected by the Romans. Today, this part of Greece produces cotton and the walls lie in ruins.

It's important to remember Philippi was a Roman colony, that all Philippians grew up under the critical gaze of people who didn't share their traditions or values and who weren't committed to their best interest. While the Philippians were often wealthy, they were still an oppressed people, under the rule and taxation of a conquering nation.

» What do you think it would be like to grow up in a colony? What might be the advantages? What would be the disadvantages?

» Sherman Alexie wrote, "Being colonized automatically makes you bipolar." What does he mean by that? How might the Philippians have been pulled into two directions?

PAUL

Paul's letter to the Philippians, deeply personal and affectionate, written in the 60s BC, is an update on Paul's current condition: he's under arrest, his life is at stake, and the kingdom of God is being blessed by his suffering. The letter is also a call to join him in his live or die posture of surrender to Christ.

It's likely you know a good bit about Paul: also called Saul, fine Jewish boy, well educated, persecuted Christians until, confronted with Christ on the road to trap Christ's followers, he had a change of heart, turned his life over to preaching the Gospel, and ended up leading Gentiles to faith (and being imprisoned and tortured) across much of the ancient world. That's Paul. He's a rockstar. We'll be spending a lot of time with him over the next few weeks.

» To get a quick glimpse at Paul's life and character, read 2 Corinthians 11: 22-33. Here Paul, responding to false teachers trying to win the favor of the church in Corinthians, offers some evidence for his authority. Read it and make a list of things you learn about Paul from the text:

» How does knowing this about Paul influence your willingness to listen to what he has to say?

THE PHILIPPIANS

While you may be familiar with Paul, perhaps you don't know so much about the church in Philippi. This church, like every church, was made up of people, normal people who bought groceries and gave their kids baths and took their shoes off at the door. These people living mostly normal lives find themselves challenged by Paul in the same way we'll feel challenged by this message of surrender and radical joy. It wasn't easier for them than it is for us. In fact, in some ways, it was much, much harder.

To get to know the Philippian church, turn to Acts chapter 16. Read verses 6-12.

» How did Paul and Silas end up in Philippi?

This is not how most of Paul's missionary journeying went. Usually Paul does his own course charting, considering where he's been, where he still wants to go, where he thinks the people might be receptive. Here though God directs Paul toward Macedonia in a clear and direct way. He hasn't directed Paul this way before (and won't again). God evidently has big plans for these people.

When Paul and Silas arrived in Philippi they didn't follow their go-to game plan of visiting the city synagogue. Most scholars think Philippi didn't have a synagogue, likely because few Jewish men lived in the city. When Paul and Silas go outside the city on the Sabbath, they find a group of women praying. As far as we know, one of these women was the first convert in the church at Philippi.

» Read Acts 16: 13-15. Who was it? What do we know about her? What did she insist upon after being baptized?

» If the Jews in Philippi were primarily women, what might that tell us about the church in Philippi?

While Lydia was the first convert in Philippi, perhaps the most dramatic conversion comes in the context of Paul and Silas' Philippian imprisonment. Having riled up the city with a miraculous expulsion of a fortune telling demon, Paul and Silas are arrested. Read Acts 16: 16-34.

While there is so much to see and discuss in this passage, let's consider particularly what it reveals to us about the character and nature of the church in Philippi:

» If Paul and Silas are imprisoned early in their ministry in Philippi, what does that tell you about the city's posture toward Christians? Would it have been easy to be a Christian in Philippi? What might early converts in Philippi have needed to consider before following Christ?

» Do you think the Philippians' posture as colonized people might have prepared them in any way to face persecution or to more fully find their identity as citizens of Heaven? How so?

» Who is converted as a result of Paul and Silas's imprisonment? How does he come to faith?

» What does the way the jailer came to Christ tell you about what kind of Christian he might have been? What did the jailer likely learn from Paul and Silas's example?

» In Acts 16:33 we read, "At that hour of the night the jailer took them and washed their wounds; then immediately he and all his household were baptized." Imagine you were the one who washed Paul and Silas's wounds. Try to see and hear and feel what it might have been like. What do you think the jailer learned about what it meant to be a Christian from washing Paul and Silas? (Hint: read Acts 16: 22-23)

The two things we must keep in mind as we read this letter to the Philippian church are: 1. Their firm understanding of what it would have meant to participate in Christ's sufferings, and 2. Their deep love for and committed partnership with the Apostle Paul.

YOU

We've talked about Paul, and we've talked about the Philippi-ans--both of whom significantly affect our understanding of this text. The last person you'll be spending a lot of time with over the course of this study is yourself. If you intend to let this study push and shape you, it's important that you enter it with a clear picture of who you are right now.

Take a minute and answer the following questions about who (and where and how) you are:

» What is your level of satisfaction with your life today--who you are and what you're doing? What's going well? Where do you feel like something's missing?

» How does the title of this study, Live or Die, make you feel? Why do you think that is? What are you hoping to learn? How are you hoping to be changed?

» Of the following virtues, which do you feel like you have and which are you lacking?

- Courage

- Trust

- Submission

- Humility

- Contentment

- Joy

Once you've answered these questions, pray that in this study God would shape you in the ways you need to be shaped, challenge you in the ways you need to be challenged, comfort you in the ways you need to be comforted and inspire you in the ways you need to be inspired.

God, lead us into transformation. Give us open minds and hearts to hear and welcome Your voice. Teach us to follow you whatever happens, live or die...

one

TO COMPLETION

"In all my prayers for all of you, I always pray with joy... being confident of this, that he who began a good work in you will carry it on to completion until the day of Christ Jesus."

READ:

Today, read verses 1-11 of Philippians chapter 1.

Remember these words are written to friends (family really) living in a largely pagan community experiencing significant persecution.

As you read, ask yourself: What did God want to say to *them* **then**? What does God want to say to *me* **today**?

FOCUS:

When I was in college I joined a social club. Social clubs were like sororities but without alcohol and with boys. As a part of this club, members wore jerseys with nicknames and numbers on the back. I didn't have a nickname so I made my name "Philippians" and my number 4:4. "Rejoice in the Lord always and again I say rejoice." Back then I thought the book of Philippians was all about joy. And it is. But, as you'll see (and as I've grown to see more clearly), it's a joy hard-won and deeply anchored in unexpected places.

Nineteen-year-old me, wearing jerseys and playing pool with

friends in the student center, was bubblier than the 36-year-old version. She giggled more, probably smiled more, too. But she didn't have half the joy of her older, more battle scarred counterpart. The joy I have today bubbles up from the springs of hardship, hard work, and partnership.

As Paul begins his letter, we see joy spilling from his pen. He so obviously loves these people to whom he's writing. Every thought of them brings him joy—despite his own circumstances. Writing from prison (possibly house arrest), probably in Rome, Paul offers his friends all he can—his blessing. For his beloved people, Paul prays for completion, that God would finish what He'd started.

Later in today's reading we find Paul praying for the Philippians, "that your love may abound more and more... so that you may be able to discern what is best and may be pure and blameless for the day of Christ, filled with the fruit of righteousness that comes through Jesus Christ—to the glory and praise of God." Notably, Paul doesn't pray for their comfort. He doesn't pray for their health or safety or happiness. He doesn't pray they'd be delivered from difficult circumstances (though they were neck-deep in suffering). He prays that they would have love, discernment, purity, and righteousness and that these virtues would shine like neon arrows pointing toward the God who gives them.

The best thing Paul could wish for his friends was that they would become what God wanted them to become and that in their full transformation God would be glorified.

As the book of Philippians unfolds we'll see, the most important thing, always and in every situation, is God's glory. The best way for God to get the glory He so deserves? When His people become what they're destined to become—loving, pure, blameless, filled with the fruit of righteousness...

Sometimes transformation like that requires suffering, as it did for both Paul and the Philippians. Always it requires self-effacing submission to the reign of God. You can't lift God up for praise and glory unless you're willing to stand below.

Paul says in verse 4, "I always pray with joy," not because things are easy for him and not because things are easy for the Philippians, but rather because they have one another, because they're partners in the gospel (vs 5), because they share God's grace (vs 7) and because they hope together, knowing one day Christ will finish His work in their hearts.

The book of Philippians is about joy, yes, but it's a collective joy that grows from stepping into your full identity and purpose alongside others who're doing the same, a joy that comes from giving up your own desires and plans, and from submitting your life's course and shape to God's authority.

THINK & DO:

Consider the following reflection questions. Grab a pen and jot down some answers.

» Is God's glory your primary goal in life? If so, great! If not, why not? Practically speaking, what would it look like for you to turn your life over as a testimony to the power and majesty of God?

» What good work has God begun in you? Look for seeds of holiness in your life. Where do you feel like God's growing you into something better? What work has God already done in you? Consider who you were five years ago. How are you different now? What did God use over those five years to shape you into the person you are now?

» Do you think of yourself as the prime mover in your spiritual growth? Or God? How do we open ourselves up to God doing good work in us? Think of some steps you could take to make yourself more available to God.

» How have you pursued joy in the past? Make a list of ways that worked and ways that didn't. Have you always understood joy as a byproduct of submission to God and partnership with others? If so, share a time when you found joy in submission—

either to God or to a partner in serving God. Does that seem strange to you—that you might find joy in giving up personal control over your life? Why or why not?

DEFINE:

(vs. 5) "Partnership in the gospel"

Here Paul is describing their participation together in the furtherance of the gospel. Jac. J. Muller says in his commentary on Philippians, "In short it refers to their sympathetic attitude and practical action in the interest of the gospel: their cooperation, zeal, prayers and sacrifice, arising from their personal appropriation of the gospel by faith."

(vs.9) "love" abounding in "knowledge and all discernment"

When we think of love we don't always partner it with things like knowledge and discernment. According to Paul, they're natural partners. Love doesn't override knowledge; knowledge is rooted in love. Here Paul is praying, in essence, "Let love be your compass and scale." Love isn't reckless or irresponsible. Love is wise and dependable.

PRAY:

Today, let Paul's prayer be your prayer. First, pray it for yourself. Second, pray it for a group of people you love, maybe your church family, your small group or a body of believers worshiping in a dark place.

"And this is my prayer... God, let my love abound more and more in knowledge and depth of insight, so that I may be able to discern what is best and may be pure and blameless for the day of Christ, filled with the fruit of righteousness that comes through Jesus Christ—to YOUR glory and praise."

WORTHY SHRIMP

Still in our pajamas eating Cheerios, my girls and I watch *Jiro Dreams of Sushi*, a documentary following the world's best sushi chef, the 85 year old Jiro Ono working in Tokyo, Japan. Every scene shimmers with precision and excellence, sharp knives glide through pink salmon, wise hands wrap fish in fluffy, sticky rice. Toward the movie's middle, Jiro's team shops at a bustling fish market, purchasers and purveyors crammed and cramped. Every vendor saves their best product for Jiro's use. On this particular day, the market is shrimp short. But there are always shrimp for Jiro.

The shrimp man says in creaky Japanese translated into English in white words at the bottom of my screen, "Sometimes I see the day's shrimp and think 'Ahhhh! This is shrimp worthy of Jiro.'"

I pause the movie, run to my desk and scrawl those words on a yellow legal pad. I read them and let them soak in: *Worthy shrimp...*

I write, "I want to be worthy shrimp."

They say you can't make quality food without quality ingredients. I wouldn't know. I'm not much of a cook. But my husband is. I watch him at the farmer's market— handling, inspecting, smelling. He picks fruit and vegetables in season, refusing to force December tomatoes into delivering what he knows they can't. Late summer is for peaches and corn. In winter we eat carrots. Squash blossoms in spring. He grows his own herbs outside our back door and pays too much money for cheese.

His food tastes like something special, something other, something right.

I am thinking of my husband's herbs and thinking of Jiro and thinking of shrimp and thinking of God and me. God doesn't require the finest ingredients to make beautiful things. Unlike Jiro, He'll work with just about anything. While Jiro can't make bad fish good, God's redemptive power is unmatched. He takes scraps and makes feasts.

Still.

God is looking for worthy shrimp—shrimp willing to be made worthy.

In Colossians 1:10 Paul prays that the church would "live a life worthy of the Lord… bearing fruit in every good work."

In Thessalonians he prays again, "that our God may make you worthy of his calling, and that by his power he may bring to fruition your every desire for goodness and your every deed prompted by faith."

And in Philippians chapter 1, he expresses confidence in a God who began a good work in His people, a God who will certainly bring it to completion, a God growing in His people the fruit of righteousness, to the glory and praise of Himself.

Somehow being in Christ, the Spirit being in us, changes our quality. When we "live a life worthy of the Lord" we're opening ourselves up to the transforming work of God. We make ourselves available to the call of God. We submit to the will of God. And in doing that, we allow God to make us worthy.

That sounds strange, maybe even heretical, to presume an ability to "allow" our sovereign God. I certainly believe God will do exactly as He pleases with whomever He pleases. But from all I've read in scripture it seems more often He prefers to work with and in the willing.

And when we're willing, He works wonders.

At Jiro's restaurant, wrapped up in seaweed, laid flat on wooden boards, you'll find only the best ingredients, the freshest fish, the finest rice. In fact, Jiro's rice source refuses to sell Jiro's favorite rice variety to any other purchaser, because when they offer up what they have to Jiro what they have is multiplied, elevated to the highest level of quality. Made perfect. People who've been say a meal at his restaurant might only last 15 minutes—he offers no appetizers, no dessert. When that happens, Jiro's meal is the most expensive per minute in the world. According to just about everybody, it's also one of the best.

The glory and the praise, of course, don't go to the rice or the shrimp. The glory goes to Jiro.

To push the metaphor to its edges, I want to be the kind of worthy ingredient that glorifies my Maker. I want people to experience the fruit God's growing in me and praise not me but Him.

two

IN CHAINS

"Now I want you to know, brothers and sisters, that what has happened to me has actually served to advance the gospel..."

READ:

Read Philippians 1:12-18. It's short. May as well read it twice.

What's clear about Paul's chains?

What's "the important thing" according to Paul?

FOCUS:

Several years ago I taught world literature at the University of Alabama in Huntsville. One afternoon during a lecture on Russian short story writers, I shared with the class that I'd lost my brother in a tragic car accident. It made sense in the moment—Russian literature is all tragic accidents—and I didn't think a thing about sharing it. After class one of my students came up to me and asked how it could be that I was doing so well. He said I seemed alive and functioning and not nearly as cripplingly sad as he was. He'd just lost his father in a car accident a few months back.

Listening to him talk I knew this was an opportunity to share the gospel, a beginning anyway, and so I prayed, "Lord, please help me not mess this up."

When he asked, "How is it that you're okay?" I said, "God."

That simple conversation over shared suffering led to a year long conversation about God and faith, a decade long friendship, and Matt's eventual conversion.

That experience, one of the most satisfying and joy-soaked of my life, taught me what Paul teaches here in Philippians 1: Suffering (even and especially) advances the gospel.

We won't all get the chance to suffer for the cause of Christ in the explicit way Paul does (if you get that chance—to be persecuted for your allegiance—be honored by it and steward it well). But many of us will have the opportunity to leverage our suffering of all kinds for the glory of God.

Nothing grows the church like bold Christians enduring hardship with peace and joy.

When you suffer, remember two things:

Your decision to suffer well—with hope, perspective and unfailing faith—will serve to advance the gospel. And...

Advancing the gospel requires you to look for opportunities to share the gospel as it plays out in your suffering story.

In other words, suffer to the glory of God.

Philippians doesn't give us a break. It doesn't say, "Hand over your life to God and you won't suffer." It doesn't say, "Hand over your life to God except when you're suffering; then you get a pass." Paul says in Philippians, *Hand over your life to God, suffering included, and in your suffering God will be glorified and you will find joy.*

THINK & DO:

Consider the following questions:

» Where/When have you seen the gospel advanced through the pain or suffering of God's people? Think of a specific example.

» Is it possible for us to get in the way of God using our suffering to transform us and reach others? What does that look like? Give an example. How can we make it easy for Him?

» Do you think about what God might be doing to redeem your pain while you're in the middle of it? How might doing that give you perspective and/or enable you to suffer well? Look back at a past experience with suffering and try to identify where God was working. What was He up to?

DEFINE

(vs. 13) "palace guard"

Though there is much debate about where exactly Paul is imprisoned as he writes this letter, most people believe Paul is writing from a Roman prison, likely after his stint under house arrest and just before his final sentencing. The palace guard (or praetorian guard) working for the Roman emperor Nero would have known Paul from their daily rotation guarding him. During that time Paul had opportunity to teach them the gospel.

(vs.18) "Whether from false motives or true, Christ is preached. And because of this I rejoice."

Verses 15 through 18 seem strange to a modern Christian audience taught to value motives as much as action. Here, Paul isn't condoning the envy at work in the hearts of these selfish and ambitious teachers (teachers trying to become bigger and more important that Paul during his absence from the church scene), but he is celebrating the truth they teach. For Paul, what matters is people hearing the gospel. Who they heard it from doesn't matter much.

PRAY:

Identify one way you're suffering right now. It might be a broken relationship, financial hardship, grief or rejection. Write about it. Come to God and ask Him to help you suffer well and to help you look for opportunities to glorify Him in your pain.

A HEALTHY DOSE OF SUFFERING

I have two daughters. They're humans, of course, and as humans they have strengths and weaknesses. Right now I'm going to tell you something that is going to make one daughter look good and one look bad. Know—it's more complicated than that. Both my kids are equally great (and not great).

My eldest daughter is brave and sturdy. She's the kind of person who wins Survivor. She eats octopus and sushi. She jumps off cliffs. She holds snakes. She can have a temperature of 102 and never complain.

My youngest daughter is different. She's more timid, cautious, and recently, alas, whiny. She visits the nurse at school on a weekly basis. She likes band-aids and air conditioning and her iPad. When we make her eat healthy food she wails like we're bathing her in hot oil.

To explain the contrast I'll use the context of a zombie apocalypse. Should there be a zombie apocalypse, London, my eldest, will survive dressed in animal furs, face painted with mud, alone in the woods with her merry band of animal friends.

Eve though, Eve is the character who dies in the first episode of the zombie show. Whining about how much she misses chicken nuggets and walking at a snail's pace, she falls behind and meets her merciful early demise.

Here's the thing: she's six. She's not brave yet. Or sturdy. But she might be one day. There's still time. And with time will come the one thing most likely to make her brave, tough, and persevering: My husband and I are praying that in Eve's life she encounters a healthy, helpful dose of suffering.

That's right, I'm praying my daughter would suffer.

Recently I was asked to talk about suffering in front of a big group of teenagers, specifically on the title "Transformed by Suffering." At first glance it's a bummer of a topic. Suffering seems sad and hard. It seems like something you avoid or fix. But, as a person who's suffered often and as a person who has walked beside many a friend in their seasons of suffering, I could say with confidence, suffering is a gift. I don't know if they bought it. But I'm pretty sure it's true.

It's what Scripture seems to say:

James says in James 1:2-4, "Consider it pure joy, my brothers and sisters, whenever you face trials of many kinds, because you know that the testing of your faith produces perseverance. Let perseverance finish its work so that you may be mature and complete, not lacking anything." According to James, suffering leads to our completion, to our fully becoming the people God intends for us to be.

Paul says in 2 Cor. 12:10, "For when I am weak, then I am strong," indicating that weakness makes way for the strength of God to work inside us, that suffering actually empowers.

Paul says earlier in 2 Corinthians, "Our light and momentary troubles are achieving for us an eternal glory that far outweighs them all." Here Paul suggests that troubles are like girl scout badges, markers of achievement, bringers of glory.

Of course Paul isn't talking about the troubles we bring on ourselves, the consequences of our own foolishness. But still, God will even use those in His efforts to transform us into the image of Christ.

Suffering, though often the product of tragedy, is a gift.

Nobody in the world is going to tell you that. They're going to tell you that suffering should be avoided at all costs. That if you're sad you should take a pill or watch Netflix or have a beer. That whatever you're feeling should be stomped out and replaced with shallow peace and temporary happiness achieved in distraction.

But we know better. And we have proof.

Consider our heroes. For me, they're people like Harriet Tubman—the Moses of her people, leading slaves out of bondage, emboldened by her years of suffering under an oppressive, life-stealing system. People like Dietrich Bonhoeffer who died a Nazi prisoner after years of leading the German church to defy those evil forces. People like Joseph in the Bible whose entire story is set in the swamps of suffering. People like my mom, an unwed mother, a teenage bride, who overcame the odds to graduate from college and raise great kids, and stay married to her husband despite the death of her mother when she was 24 and the death her 20-year-old son when she was 38.

There is something about suffering that makes heroes. The people we look up to, the people we want to be, are so often people who have walked the long, dark road of hurt and pain.

We Christians are people of the cross, following after our suffering savior. Paul says in Philippians, "I want to know Christ—yes, to know the power of his resurrection and participation in his sufferings, becoming like him in his death."

Paul desires to participate with Christ in suffering.

I can't say that's my first response when bad things happen, but I'm learning to embrace suffering as the opportunity it is.

A few weeks ago, when I spoke to the big group of teenagers about suffering and transformation, I made a list of ways I'd been shaped by years of struggling with depression. It's just one particular way I've suffered, but it serves as a good case study, an example of what God can do (and has done) with my pain. I wrote,

In depression, God has made me compassionate. I understand and have grace for other people's weakness.

In depression God has made me long-suffering. I am capable of enduring a lot, knowing that God will use it and that one day it will end.

In depression God has made me humble. I rarely get confused about where my strength comes from.

In depression God has made me disciplined, leading me into habits like Bible study and prayer upon which I depend for health.

In depression and through all my suffering, God has transformed me into someone sturdy and brave, someone not easily toppled by trouble. I've spent time in scary places and realized there's nothing to fear.

In depression God has enabled me to speak words of light and hope from a place of understanding and empathy.

I hate being depressed. If I could push a button and make my depression go away I would. I feel that way about so much of the suffering I've endured over the years—grief, loneliness, failure— and yet in weakness I've been made strong and in persevering through suffering I'm being made complete.

I don't want to suffer; I don't crave it. But I can't deny that suffering has been so, so good for making me more like Christ AND leading other people to see Christ at work in me. Like Paul, I know that "what has happened to me has really served to advance the gospel."

three

TO LIVE

"For to me to live is Christ, and to die ... g

READ:

Read Philippians 1:19-26.

Know, this isn't hypothetical for Paul. At the very moment he writes these words the emperor Nero is deciding his fate (which will ultimately be, according to historians, beheading). Try to imagine you're in a similar situation as you read. Close your eyes. What kind of room are you in? How do you feel? What are your concerns? What can you not stop thinking about?

FOCUS:

I am joining Christ in Heaven when I die. That's not a guess. It's truth. It's not arrogant or presumptuous. It's trust. God promised. I believe.

For a long time I thought you couldn't know if you were going to Heaven. I thought I might step out of line unwittingly at the last moment and blow everything. But then I read people like Paul here in Philippians, so absolutely sure of his destiny, and I realized I *could* be sure. That's why I'm not afraid to die. Not at all. To die is gain.

In Bible class a few years ago my teacher, hoping to generate some discussion, asked who was scared to die. I think he expected lots of hands, but not one went up. Not one of the fifty people in the room raised his or her hand. Maybe we were all posing because we knew the right answer was not to be scared, but I think many of us honestly weren't.

Finally, the first hand raised, but the hand-raiser had no intention of confessing fear. I looked, and the hand belonged to one of my favorite people, a girl who absolutely always speaks her mind. On this particular Sunday she was in the middle of a battle with pain medication addiction. In a few months from this moment she'd go to jail and lose custody of her kids.

When the teacher nodded her way, here's what she said—so tired of fighting the forces of evil in her life, so eager for a reset button. She said, "I don't want to sound suicidal or anything, but, well… Heck yeah, I want to die."

I love that girl.

Right there in that moment I experienced the Maranatha of the early church—the communal cry from the mouths of hungry believers, "Come, oh Lord!" In that moment we welcomed, even yearned for, the life to come.

Heck yeah.

I think "die" is the easy part of "Live or Die."

Many of us Christians have enough courage to say "to die is gain" but not enough courage (or maybe commitment) to say "to live is Christ." "To live is Christ" is hard. It means emptying your life of you. It takes perseverance, discipline, and constant sacrifice.

"To Live is Christ" says NO to the narratives we've been taught by culture and sometimes a well-meaning church:

To live is NOT to pursue my happiness.

To live is NOT to be successful and respected.

To live is NOT pleasure.

To live is NOT a happy family.

To live is NOT good health.

To live is NOT me.

"To live is Christ" means not falling in love with the world. It means holding everything in open palms—your family, your career, your health, your comfort, your financial stability—knowing none of it belongs to you, that you are entitled to nothing and deserve nothing outside the will of God. It means letting go of expectations and assumptions about how your life will play out and submitting your future to God's care.

Too, it means filling your life with God (or being filled by God), actively involving yourself in the ongoing mission of His kingdom. It means taking every opportunity to do good. It means going into all the world with the gospel. It means loving when loving is hard. It means stepping into the good works God prepared for you.

Paul can say "to live is Christ" because he knows with certainty that his life glorifies God, that the kingdom is served by his beating pulse. Can you say that?

We named this study "Live or Die" in part because it's an affirmation: no matter what, I will serve God. But it's also a call to action. Whatever you're called to do, DO IT. If it's to die, die well and without hesitation. And if it's to live (which it probably is), get up off your rump and LIVE with passion, conviction, and courage.

THINK & DO:

Spend some time in thoughtful reflection considering the following questions:

» Are you afraid to die? Why or why not? What do you lose if you die? Actually take a moment and make a list. What do you gain? Make a list here, too. Some people say, "I'm not afraid to die; I'm just afraid of what would happen to my family, what would happen to the company I've built, the church I lead, etc." Why might that kind of fear still be problematic?

» Can you say "to live is Christ"? Is your life fully surrendered to God in faithful, fruitful service? Do you see God's fruit growing in yourself? What might you still be hanging onto that you need to give up? Where do you hesitate to hand over control to God? To get a sense of that, fill in the blank in the sentence below: I could never _____.

» Do you have what Paul says he needs in order to not be ashamed—"sufficient courage"? How much courage is sufficient for Paul's situation? How do we develop courage? What's one thing you can do to grow in courage?

DEFINE:

(vs 19) "God's provision of the Spirit of Jesus Christ"

In verse 19 Paul indicates his dependence on two things: 1. The prayers of the church and 2. God's provision of the Spirit of Christ. Other versions say "the help of the Spirit of Jesus Christ" (ESV, NRSV). Paul's referring to the measure of the Spirit available to all followers of God, promised by Christ even before His death. Like Paul, we depend on the Spirit for the help we need to face difficult circumstances—what that help looks like is hard to pin down. We do know the Spirit speaks truth (John 15:26) and helps us by praying for us in a way we can't understand (Romans 8:26). Leaning into the Spirit gives us courage as we remember we're not alone.

(vs. 20) "Christ... exalted in my body"

Clearly, Paul is referring to the truth that no matter what happens, martyrdom or continued life in God's service, God will be glorified. What's interesting is Paul's use of the word "body" instead of "life." Looking back at Paul's history, we see his physical body playing a prominent part in his obedience to Christ. His body bears so many scars—from beatings, from shackles, from a snake bite, from a God-inflicted "thorn," his feet crooked and calloused from thousands of miles of travel. When Paul takes a bath, he runs his hands over bodily reminders that this vessel of skin and bones belongs to God and is used by God.

PRAY:

If you're feeling ready to offer everything up to God, to loosen your grip on every single desire, expectation, and allegiance, you're probably ready to pray the following prayer. John Wesley wrote it generations ago and since then men and women the globe over have struggled to free the words from their lips and tied tongues. I prayed it once in my car in a parking lot and cried so hard I almost threw up. Just saying. There's power here.

Shall we pray? :)

I am no longer my own, but yours.

Put me to what you will, rank me with whom you will;

put me to doing, put me to suffering;

let me be employed for you, or laid aside for you,

exalted for you, or brought low for you;

let me be full,

let me be empty,

let me have all things,

let me have nothing:

I freely and wholeheartedly yield all things

to your pleasure and disposal.

And now, glorious and blessed God,

Father, Son and Holy Spirit,

you are mine and I am yours. So be it.

And the covenant now made on earth, let it be ratified in heaven.

Amen.

HIGH STAKES

I'm watching the first episode of the zombie drama *The Walking Dead* and this character on my computer screen, a middle aged man, a father, is looking through a rifle scope from his upstairs window, trying and failing to pull the trigger and shoot his wife, his wife wandering the streets of their neighborhood in a nightgown, dead and cruelly not dead either. I can see her blank eyes as she looks up at him. I can feel his love and fear for the woman who will inevitably take his life.

That moment, watching that show for the first time, felt oddly familiar, like life sometimes feels—the choices too hard to make, the stakes too high.

Life doesn't always feel that way. Most of the time life feels like an episode of *Parks and Rec* or *Black-ish* or *Seinfeld* or *The Office*, everything small and inconsequential, a comedy of errors. Sometimes I tire of so much small.

Back when *The Walking Dead* first debuted I read an article about it and shows like it. The author, an editor at *Entertainment Weekly*, suggested that shows like this one tap into what may be the greatest fear our generation: the fear of waking up to find our entire world upturned. He said, there's nothing that scares us more than the possibility of having to start over.

As I was reading, I realized these shows he was referencing were all my favorites (*LOST, Falling Skies, Revolution*)—the kind of shows I watch not for fun but because I feel compelled, because I feel like I'm watching something important when I tune in. When I saw them boiled down so succinctly, I agreed with both the assessment of the show and the assessment of us—we do hold too tightly to things and relationships and achievement, our white knuckles the evidence of deep-seated fear. We hoard and amass and insure and diversify and deadbolt—just in case.

The Walking Dead bothers us, because it reminds us we're not in control.

So, yeah, we watch *The Walking Dead* because we're broken people, addicted to ease and luxury, safety, security and certainty. But maybe we also watch it because we long not to be. Maybe we're not just afraid. Maybe there's something more noble at work.

When I watch *The Walking Dead* I imagine myself as a character right in the middle of the action (My character-self is super tough; I wear knee-high Doc Martens and have bleached white-girl dreads—but I don't kill zombies because I'm working on an ingenuous way to heal them). When the show is on, I don't cower on the couch thinking, "I want as far away from this as possible." No, I want in.

You may not be with me on *The Walking Dead*—zombies are, admittedly, gross—so instead consider *The Hunger Games* (really any dystopic or apocalyptic drama works). You're watching Katniss with that bow and arrow, running and tree-climbing, her life ever on the line, and you're thinking what? Is it possible you're wishing you were her?

That seems crazy. Katniss—poor, tired, mentally and emotionally scarred, stuck in the middle of a devastating love triangle—is sentenced to die in a public arena to appease the blood-lust of her oppressors. And you—you want to be her?

No, of course not. But also yes. Very much, yes.

What I think is so appealing about *The Hunger Games* and *The Walking Dead* and *LOST* are the stakes. Every one of these shows (and books) suggests that in starting over, in entering a new world, these characters have stepped into something important. I think we watch and read these stories because we're tired of living small lives, and because something inside us calls out for an epic, life-threatening adventure.

I don't think we're just scared of starting over. I think we're also scared of everything staying the same.

***

It's Tuesday night and I'm sitting in my living room with my small group, my band of brothers, as we memorize a verse of scripture. We say it together aloud three times, four, five. We say it until it seems a battle cry: *If we live, we live for the Lord; and if we die, we die for the Lord. So, whether we live or die, we belong to the Lord.*

When we finished, those words burned into our beating hearts, I forgot about the emails I needed to send and the laundry piled on my bed. For a moment I remembered the high stakes life I'd chosen. Here I was at a reasonable hour on a weeknight living an epic.

A long time ago God called me to start over, to throw away what was and step into what could be. The past I left behind seemed small but it was sure, predictable, and comfortable. The future He called me to seemed big, mysterious and a little bit crazy. I picked big, mysterious and crazy.

Every once in awhile, I find myself drifting back to safe and comfortable, my life looking more like an episode of *Parks and Rec*—little at stake, small problems, easy choices. I watch *The Office* and feel comforted in a camaraderie of small living.

But then I remember the calling—"If I live, I live for the Lord; and if I die…"—and I'm drawn back into the adventure.

four

WHATEVER HAPPENS

"Whatever happens, conduct yourselves in a manner worthy of the gospel of Christ."

READ:

Read Philippians 1: 27-30. How does it make you feel?

FOCUS:

If you're reading in the NIV, today's passage begins with the words "whatever happens." The NIV is unique in this translation. Others begin with phrases like "Above all" (NLT) or "Only" (NASB, ESV), indicating the singular importance of what Paul's about to say as a response to his undetermined future. The NIV inserts "whatever happens" in an effort to emphasize his uncertainty of circumstance.

I like that. We certainly don't want to miss it.

When Paul asks this church to "live in a manner worthy of the gospel of Christ," he's asking them to do it no matter what—no excuses, no passes, no outs. That's a message the church today needs to hear.

God is glorified when His people act in ways that don't make sense given the situation. Anyone can be brave under the right set of conditions. Anyone can be patient or loving, gentle or full of faith supposing the day is good, the sea is still, and the sky is clear. It's trouble that makes virtue surprising, and it's in trouble or hardship that Christians living like Christians stand out.

Paul asks the Philippian church to conduct themselves in a way worthy of the gospel— whether or not he dies AND, as we see later in the text, whether or not *they're* called to die. Paul makes this big ask knowing that their bravery in the face of persecution would be a bright light to the world. He tells them their courage will be a sign of their salvation.

What he's asking isn't that the Philippians would be perfect, but rather that they'd conduct themselves in a way that accurately reflects their identity, their transformation in Christ and their allegiance to God. In fact, the word Paul uses for "live" or "conduct" here refers to the behavior or conduct of a citizen of a state. It's not a word Paul uses often. Here, Paul seems to be saying, "Act like a citizen of Heaven." Some translations even come out and say that explicitly: "Above all, you must live as citizens of heaven, conducting yourselves in a manner worthy of the Good News about Christ" (NLT).

Paul is simply asking the Philippians to act like the people they are, to remember where they belong and in remembering to be emboldened and empowered to face these temporary trials.

The Philippians (and you and I) are a people who have nothing to fear.

A people who face whatever comes with hope and trust.

A people who will one day reign beside God in a now-unseen, soon-to-be-revealed kingdom of glory and power.

A people who have already died once and can't die again.

God, through Paul, tells us to live like it.

THINK & DO:

Meditate on the following questions. Write down your thoughts. Then put them into action.

» How much do your circumstances affect your demeanor? Think back to the last time things went wrong. Are you the same person "whatever happens"? If not, ask God for help, and recruit some friends to hold you accountable to a new way of reacting to life's bumps.

» Are you brave? If not, why not? What are you afraid of? Make a list. Don't hold back; write down every single thing that scares you. Now, consider your list. Is there anything God can't take care of? Is there anything you don't trust God with? Pray over each item on your list, asking God to deliver you from your fear.

» How do you feel about the call to "conduct yourselves in a manner worthy of the gospel"? Is it possible? What can we do, practically speaking, to enable this in our lives?

DEFINE:

(vs 27) "worthy of the gospel"

Paul calls the Philippians to live a life "worthy" or in a manner "suitable" to the gospel. Probably what Paul means here is that his readers should live lives that match the gospel they proclaim. Peter T. O'Brien says in his commentary on Philippians that walking worthy of the gospel looks like "holding fast to it, preaching and confessing it in spite of opposition and temptation." Other commentators suggest the worthiness is evidenced by behavioral change, that this sentence stands as a sort of thesis statement for the next movement of the letter, a movement focused on internal traits like courage, love, and humility.

(vs. 28) "This is a sign to them that they will be destroyed, but that you will be saved"

While we can't be certain exactly who is persecuting the Christians in Philippi, it's likely not coming from within the church or from the Jewish community (quite small in that city). Likely, the church is experiencing pressure from pagan culture. Commentators disagree over whether Paul is saying the persecutors will recognize for themselves this "sign" in the form of the Christians' perseverance. Some suggest the opposition will see the Christians' behavior and feel God's presence in it, leading to a sense of their own damnation. Others believe the text is only indicating a sign for the Christians.

PRAY:

What do you think it looks like to live as a citizen of Heaven? Make a list of characteristics here (shoot for 10 to 15). Then pray that list, asking God to grow in you those same characteristics.

CITIZENS

I have this friend who grew up in a home with a clearly de-fined family culture. She told me one day, "In my house we knew what it meant to be a Johnson. Johnsons were winners." While she often found that identity inspiring, she also found it oppres-sive when she couldn't muster what it took to take the top prize.

My family didn't have a motto like that, but we definitely had identity markers. Mayses went to church every single Sunday, even on vacation. Mayses were devoted to the good of "the fami-ly." Mayses felt comfortable up in front of groups. Mayses rooted for either the Miami Hurricanes or the Florida State Seminoles (My parents have since changed their college football allegiance. I'm still recovering). Mayses did not hide how they felt about things. Mayses did not say "fart."

When I started dating my husband it was easy to see what made a Gerhardt: Gerhardts worked hard. *I can still hear my fa-ther in law yelling across the house, "Get up! People die in the bed!"* Gerhardts never ate fast food and never drank soda at home. Unlike Mayses, Gerhardts rarely said how they truly felt about things and often said "fart."

Every family has a culture. There are things we do and things we don't do, ways we talk, hobbies we're expected to pick up (or endure), kinds of work that are valued, other kinds that aren't.

Even when we look nothing like our family, even when we feel like we don't really belong, some gesture or saying or raw talent will slip out and give us away. These are our people and we are alike, defined by the constitution of our shared values, experi-ence, and blood.

***

At Easter, at the big feast my family hosts each year, my

husband Justin stood, glass in hand, and offered some words about caterpillars and butterflies. He said the caterpillar and the butterfly could not be more different, that even in the pupa there is no intermediate, evolutionary form that ties the two creatures together. The caterpillar dissolves inside the pupa into a gooey, protoplasmic soup, and from that soup the butterfly is born.

One thing ends and another begins.

And yet... Scientists have recently discovered that butterflies actually carry memories from their time as caterpillars, liking or disliking the same smells, for example, as they liked or disliked in their earlier form. Inside that gooey soup, scientists find cells for both the caterpillar form and the butterfly form, proving that every caterpillar is carrying around inside it all the parts it will eventually need to grow wings. Caterpillars are born with a destiny, an identity bigger and more extraordinary than their current, grounded state.

That's like us, right? Because we can be tempted to feel like the us before death and the us after death are two totally different things. That while on earth we're one way and then we die and Christ resurrects us and we're something entirely different. But the truth is that even now we're becoming. We already are the butterflies we'll become. Even now we have wings.

I see them sometimes peeking out, color flashing in the corner of my eye when I'm generous or kind, selfless or creative. I see my husband's butterfly self so often. I see butterflies in my friends at church, in my family members, in my neighbors, and in my kids.

Of course, I see the caterpillar in them, too, but it would be wrong to call them, us, caterpillars, because that's not all we are. We're both. We're becoming. We are and are about to be.

I read Paul in Philippians calling us to conduct ourselves in a manner worthy of the gospel of Christ, to live as citizens of Heaven, and I'm reminded that what I am now isn't all I'll ever be AND that I can be more now, too. I carry inside me the magic of transformation, and even today I am learning the values and rules of the kingdom to which I belong. I'm learning what it means to be a Christian, just like I learned to be a Mays and a Gerhardt. It's both in me and outside me, in the blood and in instruction; I can't help it and I'm aspiring to it—both.

Recently I went to dinner with a cousin I hadn't seen in years. She and I fell into conversation like a car off a cliff. For hours we talked and laughed. We spoke in short hand. We never misunderstood one another. That's how it is when you come from the same place, when you speak the same language, when you share the same values. Those moments of belonging, no matter where you are, feel like coming home.

I have to imagine that's what Heaven will be like: like coming home, like walking through the gates of your own country, like coming back to America after a month in Europe and ordering a Coke that comes in a 32 ounce styrofoam cup filled to the brim with ice and taking a long, luxurious sip. Familiar and perfect even after so long away.

When I get to Heaven, after years *here* becoming more and more like a person who belongs *there* I am going to look like a citizen, like I've lived there my whole life, sunning in the light of God's glory, eating the healing, whole-making fruit. I will enter His gates as a native daughter of Zion, my wings finally freed and unfurled.

five

IN HUMILITY

" In humility, value others above yourselves, not looking to your own interests but each of you to the interests of others."

READ:

Read Philippians 2:1-11. Verses 6-11 are widely believed to be hymn lyrics. If you're in the mood, try to sing them (maybe to the tune of "Amazing Grace" or some other familiar song).

FOCUS:

So far in this study we've focused on the act of emptying ourselves of self and being filled by and with God. In today's reading we discover it doesn't end there. We don't just pour out our lives so we can be filled. Once we're filled, we pour out again on the behalf of God's people. If we've handed our lives over to God, we've also handed them over to the church.

In verses one and two, Paul lists the ways the Philippian church has experienced blessing through fellowship with God. He says, "You've been encouraged. You've been comforted. You've been filled with the very Spirit of God, shown tenderness and compassion." And then, in verse three, he flips the conversation, asking the Philippians, essentially, to share—to share the mission, to share their time, to make life about us and not me.

And then he gives an example and it's not the easiest to follow because it's Jesus.

If you're anything like me, it's easy to love and serve God. Okay, not easy. Easier. Easier than loving and serving people. People disappoint me. People have thoughts that aren't my thoughts—thoughts that aren't holy and perfect like God's. People don't always show me love and compassion and tenderness. People are awkward and stubborn and forgetful and... A lot like me.

God deserves my life. *But people?*

The idea of valuing others above myself and not looking to my own interests but to the interests of others isn't the easiest thing to get my head around. It's certainly counter-cultural.

But then I see Jesus—Jesus who reigns in heaven, Jesus who IS God—I see Him stepping down to earth, divesting himself of the glory and power to which He was entitled, and serving us. Washing feet. Dying on a cross. Jesus humbled Himself to the point of death, offering up even His last breath on our behalf.

And I can't spend an hour praying for my brothers and sisters in the morning? I can't go to lunch with a widow once a week? I can't give money to my church? I can't submit in an argument? I can't put aside my own striving after success for long enough to enable and empower others to succeed?

This passage challenges me, forcing me to reconsider my me-centered life mapped in my me-focused planner with hour after hour of me-serving plans. Today, in my pursuit of a life emptied of all that doesn't matter and filled with all that does, I'm committing to look not to my own interests, but to look to the interests of others.

THINK & DO:

Consider the following questions. You might grab a pen and jot down some answers.

» What encouragement (def: being filled with courage) do you receive from being united with Christ? Give an example. Do you find comfort in Christ's love? Explain how that works.

» How do you become "one in spirit" and "one in mind" with your church family? What behaviors engender unity? What gets in the way of unity? Write down any examples from your experience.

» How good are you at looking to the interests of others? How about NOT looking to your own interests? Consider your planner and your bank statement. How much of your time and resources are you devoting to others? For a moment, don't allow yourself to look for a loophole or excuse. Just imagine what your life would look like if you gave yourself up to this command. What would change?

DEFINE:

(vs 1) "common sharing in the Spirit" or "participation in the spirit"

This appears to refer to the personal indwelling of the Holy Spirit, indicating our being gifted the Spirit or the Spirit sharing itself with us. In context, Paul asks, in essence, If the Spirit shares himself with you can you not then share yourself with the body?

(vs 2) "like-minded"

According to Peter O'Brien in his commentary on Philippians, "This verb expresses not merely an activity of the intellect, but also a movement of the will; it is both interest and decision at the same time." O'Brien suggests Paul is calling for a uniform direction—not that the Philippians should all have the same thoughts but rather that they should have a singular mission and movement.

(vs 3) "vain conceit"

This might also be translated "vainglory," the idea being that we shouldn't seek empty glory (attention or praise) for our own promotion.

(vs 6) "being in very nature God, did not consider equality with God something to be grasped."

The Greek word for "to be grasped" carries with it the idea of robbery. Thus, commentators suggest the best way to understand the passage is this: Jesus didn't consider equality with God something being stolen away from Him. It was His and He could choose to give it up if He so desired. Paul's point seems to be, if Jesus could give up what He was rightly entitled to (a position/volition equal to God's and in some way the same as God's), we can follow His example and give up our selfish desires and vain conceits.

PRAY:

For the next ten minutes pray only for other people, looking not to your own interests (you can make a list of people to pray for here). If you're up for the challenge, try not praying for yourself for a whole week. Every time you think to pray for yourself pray instead for someone else.

AT YOUR PLEASURE

Every second week of June I volunteer at my church's Champs Camp. It's basically VBS meets sports camp with the purpose of reaching our community for Christ. We're so serious about reaching unchurched kids we don't even allow our kids to come unless their parent is volunteering. Camp runs from Monday to Thursday, 9 am to 2:30 in the afternoon. Basically, all week, all day. At 2:46, when I'm released from my duty, I drive straight to McDonald's and buy a large, icy diet coke, which I inhale. Sometimes I buy two.

I appreciate Champs Camp. I love getting to know the kids. I love our crazy dance parties. I love beating a ten-year-old boy in knock out. And I love hearing stories about kids who've convinced their parents to come to church on Sunday for the first time in a long time.

But if I'm being honest, Champs Camp isn't exactly my cup of tea. It's a lot of silly, a lot of keeping track of name-tags, water bottles, who's in the bathroom… and a whole lot of interacting with people. For an introvert, Champs Camp is a challenge. For a distracted, forgetful introvert, it's like boot camp (assuming you're not in shape for boot camp and boot camp involves cheers and crafts and lots of loud songs and you don't really want to go to boot camp). What I'm trying to say is, for me, it's hard and occasionally unpleasant. I would never choose to spend my time in this way.

But I volunteer every year. I volunteer because I serve at the pleasure of Robin Marrs. More on that in a minute…

These days my husband and I can't get enough of the TV show *West Wing*. We had our first taste a few months back, and—praise be to Netflix—we've now consumed five seasons of the imagined inner workings of the White House. I almost jumped ship following the disappointing departure of Sam Seaborne, but then that thing happened with Zoey and it seemed inappropriate to leave my friends in their time of need (It's okay if you don't know what I'm talking about. But also, watch *West Wing*!).

Anyway, a few seasons back all the characters started saying this phrase. You'd hear it every time a person was called upon to do or say something they didn't want to do or say. They'd put up a fight, lose the argument, and then say, sometimes with resolve, sometimes with angst, "I serve at the pleasure of the president."

I've taken to saying it in my head when Justin asks if I would maybe, please wash a load of whites.

Back to Champs Camp...

If it were up to me, Champs Camp probably wouldn't happen. Not because I don't think it's good, but because, as we've already pointed out, it's not my thing. Fortunately, it's Robin Marrs's thing. She's our children's minister. She loves kids. She loves Jesus. She organizes with style and grace. She makes Champs Camp happen.

Robin is my sister in Christ, my partner in the Gospel at Round Rock Church of Christ. I love her. And so I volunteer for Champs Camp. Sure part of me is thinking "Do you know how many words I could have written today?" but I tell that part to shut up. Because I serve at the pleasure of Robin Marrs. Because I'm called to submission, to subjecting my own preferences and wishes to the preferences and wishes of someone else. Submission is what makes church work; it's the secret sauce in unity and cooperation and love.

Paul writes in Romans, "For just as each of us has one body with many members, and these members do not all have the same function, so in Christ we, though many, form one body, and each member belongs to all the others." He writes in Philippians, "Do nothing out of selfish ambition or vain conceit. Rather, in humility value others above yourselves, not looking to your own interests but each of you to the interests of the others." If you're anything like me, you spend a lot of time thinking about yourself—what improvements need to be made on your house, what kind of education your kids are getting, where you'll spend your vacation or how you'll spend your bonus check. I care a lot about what makes me happy. That makes sense if my life is mine. But it's not. When we're a part of a body, what's mine is yours and what's yours is mine:

If someone at your church loses everything in a fire, your couch is her couch.

If a crying baby needs to be held in the nursery, your arms are his arms.

If the elders ask you to give more generously, your money is their money.

If a widow needs a friend, your time is her time.

And if a friend plans an event to reach a bunch of people with God's love, your week is her week.

It's like that song, "I belong to you, You belong to me..." Submission says, "I serve at the pleasure of the body."

In an hour or so I'll head to this year's Champs Camp. I'll arrive at a building full of people, many of whom are perky morning people. There will be much smile-screaming. I may have to walk through a human tunnel. I will likely turn in circles as I hop on one foot with my tongue stuck out. I will probably be doused with water. And I will love it. Not because I love screaming and water balloons and ridiculous kids' songs (I don't). I'll love it because my brothers and sisters love it and because I love my brothers and sisters and because I "belong to all the others."

six

WITHOUT GRUMBLING

*"Do everything without grumbling or arguing, so that
you may become blameless and pure..."*

READ:

Read Philippians 2:12-18.

Find a phrase that jumps off the page. Write it here. Why do
you think that sticks out to you so much?

FOCUS:

This year I made exactly one resolution. I figured if I made
just one I'd be more likely to keep it. I'd have more energy to in-
vest in it. I'd be more focused. I'd be more likely to succeed. How
hard could keeping one resolution be?

Um, hard.

This year I resolved to stop complaining. I am blowing this
resolution right and left.

Honestly, I didn't expect it to be this hard. I thought I could
just turn it off like a water faucet. No more complaining. No
problem. But what I realized was that complaint for me wasn't
crankiness or impatience. It was more complicated than that. For
me, complaining had become a language of manipulation...

I complain when I want people to know how hard I'm trying.
It gets me attention and affirmation.

I complain when I've messed up but don't want others to see my failure as all my fault. It gets me off the hook.

I complain when I feel like I deserve or am entitled to better. It gets me what I want.

If I don't complain, how will I ever get what I want?

THAT is the yucky struggle in my heart. I want what I want.

Paul mentions arguing here, too. Argument is so similar to complaint in that it's largely selfish. I argue because I want to be heard. Because my opinion matters. Because I know more or better. Because I deserve attention and respect.

When Paul urges the Philippians not to grumble/complain or argue/dispute, he's tapping into the same message he's been pounding into our heads for two solid chapters: Stop thinking about you. It's not about you.

This is SO counter cultural. Paul says, if you can just get this into your head—it's not about me—you will inevitably stand out. You'll be like a star shining against a backdrop of pitch black, fundamentally and materially different from the world.

That is what God intends for His tribe—radical selflessness that stands in sharp relief against the selfish world, bringing glory (and people) to God.

THINK & DO:

Grab a pen and work through the following questions. Let's give this our full attention.

» Are you a complainer? Try to be real with yourself. Do you often find yourself dwelling on disappointments, problems, road blocks? Do you regularly point out the ways other humans are offending you? Try to remember the last time you complained. What were you complaining about? What do you think that reveals about you (if anything)?

» If you're convicted by this call from God to STOP the complaining, make sure you do two things: 1. Pray asking God to help you overcome your tendencies. 2. Ask someone close to you to hold you accountable. You should pick someone right now. For real. Don't go on to the next question until you've sent a text asking for help. Write their name below.

» Are you an argue-er? If you're having a hard time deciding, consider your behavior on social media. Do you feel compelled to "correct" others (or at the very least "weigh in") when you disagree with them? In conversation, do you often "correct" your friends or spouse when they get small details of a story wrong? When you're in an actual conflict, do you care more about resolving the problem or winning—being heard, respected, and agreed with? Would you call yourself "submissive"? Use these questions to figure out whether or not you need to make some changes in the way you approach relating to others (and possibly to God). Write out your thoughts below.

» Does the idea of standing out from the culture around you make you uncomfortable? If so, think of a friend for whom it seems effortless. Make an appointment to sit down with her and ask questions. In what direction do you feel like God might be calling you to make your next countercultural step?

DEFINE:

(vs. 12) "work out your salvation with fear and trembling"

First "work out your salvation"—This phrase could also be translated "bring about or create" your salvation, but that translation gives rise to just as many questions as the other. As we've already seen in chapter 1 of Philippians, salvation is God-given. So, what does it mean that we "work it out"? While commentators disagree (some suggest Paul is referring to some sort of corporate, church-wide "well-being" as opposed to a "personal" literal "salvation") it seems most accurate to understand this phrase as an urging for saved people to keep living like saved people. Commentator Peter T. O'Brien paraphrases Paul's meaning this way: Paul commands the Philippians to make their ultimate and eventual salvation "fruitful in the here and now... [which will involve] a continuous, sustained effort." O'Brien says working out our salvation looks like "the outworking of the gospel" in our day-to-day living. Numerous times in his writing Paul ties behavior on earth to later salvation, but few scholars are willing to suggest a direct correlation between the two. While I'm no scholar, I struggle to understand this passage outside that paradigm.

Okay, "fear and trembling"—This phrase comes directly from

the Old Testament, used again and again to describe the appropriate reaction to close physical proximity to God. It does, in fact, mean literal trembling. O'Brien says it means "an awe and reverence in the presence of the God who acts mightily." He argues Paul is looking ahead to man's final face-to-face meeting with God, suggesting that the Philippians act now in light of that day.

(vs. 17) "poured out like a drink offering on the sacrifice and service coming from your faith"

Here Paul is using a metaphor to describe the relationship between his sacrifice of his life and the Philippians' sacrifice of their lives. The comparison is to "libations" or drink offerings poured on top of sacrifices in pagan practice or around the base of the altar in Jewish practice. Paul simply means to emphasize their partnership or togetherness in giving all to Christ.

PRAY:

Think of a circumstance or situation that's been tempting you to complain or argue in recent days. Bring it to God. Look for ways to thank and praise Him for (or in) that situation or circumstance.

Example: *God, I'm tempted to complain about the money being tight. Thank you for sustaining us even in lean times. Thank you that there is always enough food. Thank you for teaching us to depend on you. Thank you for a church family that helps when we're in need... etc.*

GIVING SOMETHING UP

Parenting is like herding cats. I don't know who first said that to me, someone wise and honest (my favorite kind of person), but I know I heard it more than once and I know I say it twice a day. *Herding. Cats.*

This is especially true when you have to get your kids out of the house and into a car. If I could outsource one part of parenting, that would be it. I would hire some nice, unsuspecting person (or maybe a very smart sheepdog) whose entire job consisted of overseeing the evacuation of my house and car incarceration for children.

You can imagine how it usually goes: Lots of me screaming, "It's time to go!" Lots of reactive screaming: "I can't find my shoes!" "Eve stole my backpack!" "I hate those shoes!" "London lost Leo (the pet rat)! "I don't waaaaant to go!" When the front door finally closes behind us, odds are somebody's crying, somebody's forgotten their shoes, and somebody left her keys on the counter.

Next comes crossing the yard, navigating treacherous hazards like fire ants, wind, a too-sunny sun or, Heaven forbid, rain. Things will be dropped. Children will casually plop down and pick flowers. Mother will whisper-yell.

When we arrive at the car, the hardest part is still to come: seat belts. My children do not willingly accept self restraint. They will sit in the wrong seat. They will argue over who sat in what seat last. They will say they cannot, just cannot put on their seat belts. There will be much drama. And much use of the word "consequences." And sometimes, the administration of said consequences.

[Insert long, resigned sigh.]

One day, after a particularly rough house extrication and car loading, I looked in my rear view mirror and said, "Do you girls know how much it would mean to me if once, just once, you'd get ready and walk to the car and put on your seat belts without whining and without Mommy having to beg?"

London said, "I'm sorry mom."

Eve said, "I love you."

And I said, "If you loved me, you'd obey me," and threw the car into reverse. Because that's the kind of mother I am.

If my kids, four and five, really loved me, they'd put on their shoes and walk to the car and buckle their own stupid seat belts. Because it's easy enough to do, and because it would mean the world to me. Don't give me any of that "they're still little" junk. They know better. Best believe that.

When I read Jesus say, "Anyone who loves me will obey my teaching," I feel him. Because to love someone is to listen to her and to know her and to want (deep down) to bless her. My kids may love me with kisses and hugs and giggles—fun things to share—but they're getting old enough to start sacrificing for love, to choose me over their laziness, to choose my happiness over their own.

I tell my girls, love is giving something up for someone else. And of course I'm talking to myself as much as I'm talking to them, because I don't always like giving things up either.

When I look at my children being disobedient and contrary, I see me—me whining, pretending to read a book, or just sitting on the couch with no shoes while God tries to drag me out the door. He's probably taking me somewhere great. I know that's usually what I'm trying to do for my kids. He's probably going to feed me or show me something beautiful or teach me something.

But I want what I want. And I act like a four year old, and either don't obey or go kicking and screaming.

Maybe I'm wrong, but I think most of us want to do what we want to do. And so we choose a church that'll let us think what we already think. Or skip church because it makes us uncomfortable. We choose friends who do what we like to do and say the same things we like to say with houses exactly as nice as our own and movie taste like ours. And all along we're just doing what we like, never considering that maybe it isn't what God wants for us, that maybe loving God takes giving something up.

Sometimes God's yelling "It's time to go" and we're acting like we can't hear Him over the noise of the TV, making excuses, arguing, and otherwise dawdling in a sort-of-passive, sort-of-active disobedience. I wonder if God the Father looks over at Jesus, shakes His head, and says, "Herding. Cats." To which the Spirit, I'm sure, says, "You have no idea."

I don't want God shaking His head at me. I don't want Him to feel ignored. I don't want Him wishing I'd just do what He says. I don't want to complain and talk back. What I want is to love Him. I want to make sacrifices for Him. I want to listen to Him. Even when I don't want what He wants, I want to do it anyway.

A few weeks ago I was getting ready to take the girls somewhere. As I finished brushing my hair, I yelled the usual "It's time to go." I heard scurrying, and then the front door slammed closed. I stepped out of my room and into the living room and couldn't find the girls anywhere. I walked outside. Nowhere. And then to the car. I opened the back car door, and there, sitting in their car seats, buckled and smiling so big, were my two girls. London looked at Eve. Eve giggled. London looked back at me. She said, "We love you, Mom."

And I said (crying of course), "I know you do."

seven

AS RUBBISH

" Indeed, I count everything as loss because of the surpassing worth of knowing Christ Jesus my Lord.

For his sake I have suffered the loss of all things and count them as rubbish, in order that I may gain Christ"

READ:

Today, read verses 1-16 of Philippians chapter 3.

This is a longer reading than usual. Be sure to underline or highlight any spots that stick out or cause you to scratch your head. Write any questions you have here.

FOCUS:

A few years ago I was feeling super... small. I'd been a big accomplish-er for most of my youth. I'd won lots of awards. I'd done very well in school. And now I was writing articles no one read on the Internet and changing diapers. I felt unimportant.

So I got out all my old awards. I got out my SAT scores and college transcripts, piled it all on the living room floor. And for a second I felt better. My husband came home from work, and I told him what colleges I'd been recruited to after high school (he already knew, of course). I ran through the list with this big, confident smile on my face. Then I told him what I'd been do-ing—how I'd been struggling to feel important, and about how I was feeling a little better now—like I'd been reminded I matter. His reaction surprised me. He seemed unimpressed and disappointed.

A few weeks later, back to feeling unimportant, I complained to my husband. I said, "I feel so small."

And he looked at me with love in his eyes and said, "That's because you are."

Ouch. *In a good way.*

For way too long, waaaaayyy too long, I thought I mattered because of me. I'd been taught self-confidence from childhood, and I'd excelled at it, working hard to become a person I could respect. I dressed well. My hair always looked great. I did exceedingly well at school and work.

Then I had kids. I gained weight and wore messy clothes and didn't "work" at all. Suddenly all that confidence evaporated. Self confidence always does disappear eventually. Selves are not worthy of confidence.

Paul tells us in chapter 3 of Philippians, You are not great because of you. No matter how great you might have been, it's not enough. AND until you stop trying to find value in who you are and what you've done, you won't ever be able to gain Christ, to share in his sufferings and attain to the resurrection of the dead.

Specifically here Paul is identifying his past reasons for religious self-confidence, calling out those who want Christians to adhere to the old law system, finding righteousness in their own moral perfection instead of in Christ.

I've tried that, too. Tried to pile up service and disciplines into a mound of memorized scripture, Bible class student of the year trophies and perfect church attendance that would hopefully reach the gates of Heaven. The pile was never enough, and I wore myself out building it.

Later in this passage Paul says, "Forgetting what is behind and straining toward what is ahead, I press on toward the goal."

Paul reminds us to live now—to forget what we've done in the past (good or bad) and keep chasing Christ. Our past accomplishments (and failures) only weigh us down when we drag them behind us like luggage without wheels.

Let it go. Move on. Remember, everything is trash compared to the greatness of knowing Christ. You'll never regret placing your confidence completely in Him.

THINK & DO:

Reflection question time. You know the drill:

» Do you have reasons to put confidence in the flesh? Go ahead and make a list like Paul's. Before (outside) Christ, what made you awesome/worthy/special? Look at your list. Now think about these words from Paul: "I consider them rubbish that I may gain Christ." Are you holding on to any of your accomplishments, finding identity and confidence in those things? Ask God to help you turn them over. Start by tossing your list in the trash.

» Do you feel like knowing Christ is a "surpassing greatness"? If so, take a minute to write down what that feels like, how it plays out in your life. How is Jesus making your life great? If not... I find a lot of people struggle to relate to Paul's experience in Christ because they've never fully leaned into that kind of relationship. What might you need to do or change in order to truly "know Christ and the power of his resurrection and the fellowship of sharing in his sufferings"?

» Let's memorize some scripture! I know, I know—memorization isn't everybody's cup of tea. BUT I really think you'd be blessed by committing verses 7-8 and 10-11 to memory. Sometimes you need to give yourself a speech, a kick-in-the-pants reminder of who you are and what matters. Having these words inside you, accessible whenever you need them, would be so helpful. Do the hard work of getting them in your head. Future You will be thankful. Write them below to get started.

DEFINE:

(vs. 2) "those dogs... those mutilators of the flesh"

The "dogs" Paul refers to here are Jewish Christians who teach that all Christians must be circumcised to be a part of the family of God. These teachers regularly visit the churches Paul establishes on his missionary journeys, always after he's left, in an attempt to correct Paul's teaching. They drive Paul crazy. Here Paul uses the very word they use for Gentiles to describe them—"dogs" being unclean and "outside" the people of God.

(vs.14) "for the prize of the upward call of God in Christ Jesus"

This could be interpreted a number of ways. Some commentators suggest this language references the practice of an emperor at the end of a race calling the winner "upward" to his seat in the arena for commendation. This was, in fact, a common practice in Greece and Rome. Others don't see that metaphor in the text and simply suggest a more literal meaning—Paul being "called" or "drawn" into a deeper relationship/fellowship with Christ.

(vs. 16) "Only let us hold true to what we have attained"

Literally this passage means to "stand in line" or "march in line" with the truth we already know. Paul is encouraging the Philippians to keep going and reaching, of course, but in that forward progress to keep doing the good they know to do, together in formation. He's saying, in essence: as a united body, hold your ground.

PRAY:

If you're willing, pray this prayer derived from our reading today:

God, Maker, Sustainer, Ruler of Everything,

Whatever I might count as gain, I count as loss for the sake of Your Son, my Savior, Christ.

I count everything as loss because of the surpassing worth of knowing Christ Jesus my Lord.

For His sake, help me, God, to suffer the loss of all things and count them as rubbish, in order that I may gain Christ and be found in Him.

Help me not to rely on a righteousness of my own but to welcome and stir up the righteousness that comes through faith in Christ, the righteousness that comes from You and depends on faith.

Strengthen my faith.

I want to know Christ and the power of His resurrection. Lead me to share His sufferings, and become like Him in His death through my sacrificial living.

God, by any means possible, enable me to grab hold of the resurrection from the dead.

HOW TO BE THE YOU YOU MOST WANT TO BE

I'm dropping off my daughter at art class fully decked out in her personally-chosen, perfect-for-who-she-is Halloween costume. She decided to be a fawn this past spring (we talk Halloween costumes year round in this house) and never wavered on the choice. She likes gentle, beautiful animals. Most of the time she's pretending to be one or catching one. We spent an hour this morning doing her makeup. When she jumped out of the car she looked just like a baby deer— furry belly, perky ears, white tail that bounces as she walks, white spots like freckles on her now brown cheeks.

I am swooning. Not just because she looks beautiful (breathtaking, really), but also because she looks so much like herself, like London Jane's inside turned outside.

Isn't that a big part of what life's about, trying to get what's inside (the good stuff, anyway) to bloom, to manifest on the outside?

Every year I tell my girls when we plan Halloween costumes, "Be who you want to be." I don't show them a catalog. We don't go to the costume aisle in Target. We brainstorm, and I welcome almost every idea. Within my two rules (1. We will not glorify death or evil and 2. We will not expose our bodies), nothing is too far-fetched. If you really want to be a fawn or Indian warrior or Glinda the Good Witch—that is what you'll be. Their choices spring from dreams, aspirations, fantasies, and their personal sense of identify.

Now, this way of doing things isn't easy. Especially since I can't really sew. It's inconvenient. It involves brainstorming meetings with the kids, sketches, multiple shopping trips, scavenging sessions at Goodwill, and late nights with a glue gun. It's not for everybody. But for me, it's a chance to teach a really important lesson. I'm trying to use this small thing to show them something big: that they don't have to pick who they want to be from a small list of uninspired choices, that dreams don't come in convenient packages, that identity is something God grows inside us, not something we shop for at Target.

I want them to know it will never be easy to be who you want to be, but it will always, always be worth it.

I've noticed we adults are often bad at being who we want to be. We make excuses. We're not creative. We pick pre-packaged identities and try to cram ourselves in. We choose what's easy instead of what we know we could and should be.

Think about it for a second. Who do you want to be? If you could suddenly transform into the ideal version of yourself, what would it look like?

It's possible you have the answer right on the tip of your tongue. It's possible you think about this a lot. Some of us don't. Either way, thinking about it or not thinking about it, there is too often too big a gap between who we want to be and who we are.

Christians feel this tension just like everybody else. In fact, in some ways we feel it more. Because out of all the people, we know most clearly what's "best." We know (or should know) what could be, but we regularly settle for less. We see mediocre versions of the life Christ calls us to and instead of wanting more, we do what's required to blend in, thankful for the excuse not to try harder.

We read the Bible and see radical generosity. But we don't really want to do the hard work of figuring out how that would look in our lives so we grab a ten percent tither costume off the rack and call it a day.

We think maybe our life is too crammed with things that don't matter and not crammed enough with the Spirit of God so we drop a show from our weekly line-up of TV watching and buy a book with 365 daily devotionals, readable in two minutes or less.

Maybe we know we're buying too much so we give away our extra, donate three bags of clothes to charity, but we never change the way we're buying, never root around in our hearts to figure out what hole we're trying to fill with all this stuff, and so we keep buying irresponsibly and single-handedly stocking Goodwill. Isn't that great?

Maybe we want to love more and better so we do the stuff that makes us feel good like paying for the person behind us in the Starbucks line while continuing to avoid the stuff that makes us uncomfortable, the stuff that might push us and grow us like forgiving our addict sister or the dad who left when we were little.

Way too many of us Christians are settling for a mediocre version of ourselves, wearing ill-fitting costumes that itch and pull.

I see you yanking at the collar. I know you want more.

What does more looks like? Who are you going to be?

***

In Philippians chapter 3 the apostle Paul writes about his own desire to be made into the man Christ wants him to be. He says, "Not that I have already obtained all this, or have already arrived at my goal, but I press on to take hold of that for which Christ Jesus took hold of me. Brothers and sisters, I do not consider myself yet to have taken hold of it. But one thing I do: Forgetting what is behind and straining toward what is ahead, I press on toward the goal to win the prize for which God has called me heavenward in Christ Jesus."

What is Paul trying to take hold of, exactly? If you look back two verses you can find it: "that I may gain Christ and be found in him, not having a righteousness of my own that comes from the law, but that which is through faith in Christ—the righteousness that comes from God on the basis of faith." Paul's goal is Christ-born, faith-founded righteousness. He wants to be a better version of himself, the version Christ died to enable. He wants it, AND he's going to do what it takes to get it.

Here's what I can learn from Paul here in Philippians about being the me I want to be:

1. I have to have faith.

God's vision for you is spectacular, but know you can't achieve it without Him. When you come to God, when you surrender your will, His Spirit takes root in your heart and begins the work of transformation. When we trust God to shape us He will. But remember, trust is active. Trust does what God asks. If I have faith that God will make me the person He wants me to be, I have to actually do what God wants me to do.

2. I have to forget what's behind.

Paul had both good things and bad things to forget. He forgot his accomplishments and position as well as the dark, God-defying acts in his past. If I want to be the me I want to be, I'm going to have to stop looking back, to let go of my past achievements and get over my guilt—both of which are like millstones around my neck, making every step forward much harder than it has to be.

3. I have to strain toward what's ahead.

Straining toward what's ahead is simply persevering in hope—it's doing hard work with confidence it will eventually pay off. Yes, being the me I want to be is difficult, but the transformation, the blooming of my Christ-shaped heart, is so worth the blood, sweat, and tears. Embrace the spiritual disciplines, welcome trials, be courageous and take risks, ask hard questions, do things that make you uncomfortable, make commitments—and do all of it knowing it's leading to the "prize for which God has called [you] heavenward in Christ Jesus."

You probably know who you want to be, who you really want to be. Go ahead, follow Paul's example and be her. Be him.

If you don't know, figure it out. But figure it out with God, far away from the catalog of options dished out by a world offering only extra small and small sized dreams. Don't settle for some desaturated, vanilla version of you that looks more like the Target Halloween costume than the real thing God has planned. Be creative and courageous with your dreams, and be diligent and determined in partnering with God to make them real.

eight

IN HEAVEN

"But our citizenship is in heaven. And we eagerly await a Savior from there, the Lord Jesus Christ"

READ:

Read Philippians 3:17-4:1. Read slowly.

Are you a citizen of heaven? Or are you an enemy of the cross?

FOCUS:

Today's short reading includes several challenging and helpful truths. Paul emphasizes the power of following good examples. He encourages us to keep our eyes open for enemies of the cross, including a checklist for easy identification:

Is their god their belly?

Do they glory (or seek attention and praise) in what's shameful?

Are their minds set on earthly things?

Here he also reminds us of our identity (citizens of Heaven) and our destiny (complete transformation by the power of Christ).

All of those truths (some we've already considered in depth) are worthy of reflection. Personally I find myself compelled by the line "from it [Heaven] we await a Savior, the Lord Jesus

Christ" in verse 20.

We await...

I am a person who struggles to navigate imperfection. All day long I am disappointing my own idealism, doing what I don't want to do, not doing what I do want to do. I am frustrated by the impossibility of making this place, even this individual life, a Heaven. My perfectionism is undeniably unhealthy, and I'm working on how to handle it. That being said, I think it grows out of something that's not so wrong. I think, deep down, I'm just longing for home, itching in this ill-fitting flesh.

What does it look like to wait for a savior? I think it has something to do with not settling for a cheap version of one. I think waiting for a savior means not accepting the way things are, keeping in the forefront of our minds our need for rescue. I think it means not following the masses in gluttony and not seeking fame for what should be embarrassing. I think it means refusing to allow distractions to temper our hunger for what's coming. I think it means being okay with not getting "results" in the here and now, deciding to wait it out, to keep doing the right thing knowing eventually it will pay off.

Lately waiting is unpopular among Christians. We talk a lot about Heaven breaking through *now*, about Heaven on earth as God's ultimate plan. I'm all about the kingdom coming into lives and situations. I believe God works here. He hasn't abandoned us. BUT I also believe firmly that this place is not my home. And no matter how good it gets, my posture as a child of God is one of active waiting. Waiting on a rescue. Waiting on a Rescuer.

THINK & DO:

Consider the following questions. Grab a pen and jot down some answers.

» Do you have people in your life who "walk according to the example"? List two or three people you're following after as they follow Christ. What are you learning from their examples?

» Is it possible you're living as an enemy of the cross? Consider the following diagnostic questions:

> Are you serving your most base impulses like hunger, lust, and greed?

> Do you overeat, seek sexual satisfaction in inappropriate places, rely on money for happiness?

> Are you reveling in sin (bragging about it on Instagram) that should bring you shame?

> When was the last time you excitedly told someone about something you'd done that you knew was wrong?

> Are you setting your mind of the stuff of this world? List three things you've been thinking too much about this week.

Don't assume the answer is no. Ask God to help you see the truth. If you've positioned yourself as an enemy of the cross, be sure to pray to God and confess. Ask Him for forgiveness and strength to step into your true identity. Also, confess to a friend. Get some help as you try to realign your allegiance.

» Would you say you're actively waiting for Jesus to return? What does that look like in your life? What should it look like? How does Jesus' eventual return affect your today?

DEFINE:

(vs. 19) "they glory in their shame"

Paul's language here suggests he's referring directly to people who boast or are proud of their sexual sins, sins Paul thinks should be embarrassing.

(vs. 21) "the power that enables him even to subject all things to himself"

Christ's divine power is such that in the final transformation of mankind, Christ subjects the entire universe to himself. Your savior is all-powerful, in charge of everything. And when He comes to save you, His power will come into its full fruition.

PRAY:

Today, in prayer, tell God why you're looking forward to Heaven. You might make a top ten list of reasons.

Too, pray that the kingdom of Heaven would come (in small measure) before Jesus' return through the actions and words of God's people.

1.

2.

3.

4.

5.

6.

7.

8.

9.

10.

WAITING

When I was ten years old, two girls in my fourth grade class invited me to go to the movies. I'd never in my entire life *ever* been to the movies with friends. These girls weren't friends exactly. They were better than friends; they were popular.

I went home, put on my favorite denim vest and jeans, curled my bangs, applied a bottle of hairspray and sat on my grandmother's hibiscus print couch in the living room waiting to be picked up, my hands on my knees, my back straight, the curtains pulled from the window so I could watch the street.

My memories of that night are the colors of sunset, first gold, then pink, then purple. *Gray turning to midnight blue.* I remember my mother tenderly turning on the lamp by my side, its light cutting a path across the brown shag carpet. I didn't move from the third couch cushion for three hours. The girls never came, but I waited until my mom called me to bed.

That night on the couch I waited for something that would never come; I watched a robust and sure hope, bubbling-over joy, dissolve into crushing despair.

Sometimes I feel that way while I'm waiting for God, like I'm looking out a window down an empty street as the sun sets on my hope.

Christians are a waiting people. Our eager anticipation of something to come defines us and drives us. Jude writes, "But you, dear friends, by building yourselves up in your most holy faith and praying in the Holy Spirit, keep yourselves in God's love as you wait for the mercy of our Lord Jesus Christ to bring you to eternal life" (Jude 1:20-21).

Paul says to Titus, "For the grace of God has appeared that offers salvation to all people. It teaches us to say "No" to ungodliness and worldly passions, and to live self-controlled, upright and godly lives in this present age, while we wait for the blessed hope—the appearing of the glory of our great God and Savior, Jesus Christ" (Titus 2:11-13).

James: "Be patient, then, brothers and sisters, until the Lord's coming. See how the farmer waits for the land to yield its valuable crop, patiently waiting for the autumn and spring rains. You too, be patient and stand firm, because the Lord's coming is near" (James 5:7-8).

I look at those people in the first century, so sure He'd be back any moment, and I want that kind of urgent hope, that kind of right-around-the-corner certainty. But I have two thousand years between me and them and those years dull the clarity that came from Christ-proximity. I've never seen Jesus; so when I imagine Him returning I can't see His face or hear the tenor of His voice. Too, I've been waiting longer than they did, their wait stacked on top of generations of waiting stacked on top of mine. I bear the burden of a hope deferred for generations.

I, like you perhaps, have devoted my entire life to waiting. And if the thing I'm banking on doesn't happen, it will all have been a waste.

If only for this life we have hope in Christ, we are of all people most to be pitied.

***

My Nana is in her eighties. She grew up in southern Illinois and has rooted for the Chicago Cubs her whole life. Growing up, I saw Nana watch hundreds of baseball games, usually with the sound off, sometimes on the TV in the living room while Poppa watched his beloved Cardinals on the TV in the den, both of them decked out in team colors. Over the course of their marriage (and rivalry) Poppa's cardinals won five world series titles.

Over the course of her eighty plus year life the Cubs won none.

And still Nana rooted for the Cubs. She has been a most devoted (and disappointed) fan.

So when the Chicago Cubs won the World Series, and the whole city, like a long-dormant volcano, erupted in joy, I cried. I cried because my Nana and a tribe of fans all over the country, saw their wildest dream come true.

The longer you wait for something, the less likely it seems to ever happen, and the sweeter it is when it does.

Yesterday I started reading the book of Joshua. When Joshua takes charge after Moses dies, God's people the Israelites, have been wandering in the wilderness for forty years. Now, all their older relatives having died off, Joshua leads a group of people who've never known anything other than the mountains and deserts of the Sinai Peninsula. They've heard stories about their parents' God, about a split sea and plagues. They believe those stories; they're loyal to that God. But still, all they know is the wandering. They're unacquainted with victory and the fulfillment of promises.

They're the Cubs of the Old Testament.

Then God tells Joshua it's time, time to leave the wilderness, time to take the Promised Land, and Joshua tells the people to get ready. In chapter 3 Joshua gives instructions for how they'll cross the Jordan River. He tells them to follow the ark of the covenant, "Then you will know which way to go, since you have never been this way before."

Since you have never been this way before.

Just thinking about those kids playing on one side of the river their whole lives, skipping rocks to the other side, those kids now young adults looking beyond the river, wondering what's coming for their families, daydreaming about planting a vineyard on their own plot of land, wondering what grapes taste like—all of it makes my heart skip a beat.

This is what they've been waiting for.

In the next few chapters God will miraculously dam the Jordan, allowing them to cross on dry land. He'll show up in their camp and talk face to face with their captain. He'll knock down the walls of the fortified city of Jericho and enable their total victory. They'll eat grapes and honey.

What must that have been like? For a Jewish girl who'd never known anything beyond a refugee camp in the desert, who'd never tasted anything other than her daily rations of manna and quail, who'd spent her whole life in a holding pattern, waiting for her parents and grandparents to die so she could move on, a girl who'd never seen the miracles of which she'd heard stories.

What would it be like to see your wildest dreams come true?

One friend of mine, a Chicagoan, said that on the night the Cubs won the World Series the church bells in her neighborhood rang as if God Himself were celebrating with her loyal, persevering city.

I thought of all the things I'm hoping for, all the things I'm dreaming that haven't happened yet, all the promises God's made that aren't quite fulfilled and I imagined they had been and my heart swelled as I listened to the church bells and watched the walls of Jericho tumble.

This morning, I'm thinking of my friends and family, all of us waiting for something impossible. I'm thinking about friends in marriages that seem too broken to fix, friends estranged from parents, friends trying and failing to meet professional goals, friends trying and failing and trying again to become the people

God wants them to be, and all of us waiting for the return of our rescuing Savior. I'm thinking of us and thinking of Israel and thinking of the Cubs losing for a century and feeling like maybe it's a good idea to persevere even when something seems like it's never going to happen.

My second daughter came a week after her due date. The night before I went into labor, exasperated by the wait and unsure she'd ever decide to come out, I wrote, "Why is it that every day that passes makes me more uncertain this child will ever come? Doesn't each passing day make it more likely she'll come tomorrow?"

We've all waited a long time for Christ's return. Longer than makes logical sense. But in our waiting we've been carried, fed, healed, loved, led. We Christians wait wading in words of love and promise, assertions of God's faithfulness to His pilgrim people:

"Let us hold unswervingly to the hope we profess, for he who promised is faithful" (Hebrews 10:23).

"We have this hope as an anchor for the soul, firm and secure" (Heb 6:19).

"Those who hope in me will not be disappointed" (Isaiah 49:23).

Waiting on God has been nothing like that lonely wait on my couch years ago. I wait in community. I wait in joy. I wait in founded hope. I wait not by the fading light of a setting sun but rather by the growing light of a rising one.

nine

IN EVERYTHING

"Do not be anxious about anything, but in everything by prayer and supplication with thanksgiving let your requests be made known to God. And the peace of God, which surpasses all understanding, will guard your hearts and your minds in Christ Jesus."

READ:

Read Philippians 4:4-9. These verses will likely be familiar. Look for something you haven't noticed before.

FOCUS:

Do not be anxious about anything...

For some of you those words don't seem helpful. They seem like a locked door you've tried to open a hundred times. They seem heavy, like a bag of bricks you carry on your sagging shoulders. They seem like an accusation. You don't want to be anxious. Who wants to be anxious?! But you *are* anxious.

You wonder, "How could God ask me to do something I can't do?"

Think for a sec about all we've covered so far. Paul's told us, Don't be afraid to die for Christ. Hand over your whole life. Let God do whatever He wants in you. Put others before yourself. Be pure and blameless. Don't complain. And live a life worthy of the gospel.

These are big things. Things you can't do. Not alone.

I know anxiety seems impossible to put down. It is. And it isn't.

Paul is offering you another way here. He says, Pray about it. Ask God to intervene. Thank God for what He's done in the past as you anticipate with trust and hope what He'll do in the future. And then he promises the peace of God.

The promise here isn't that you won't ever be tempted to worry. It's not that you'll never have another anxious thought. The promise is that so long as you're handing everything over to God, thanking Him and trusting Him, peace will guard your heart and mind. Imagine peace as a bouncer at the door of your attention, letting in what's good and keeping out what's not. It's a wonderful system, but it requires you staffing the door. You have to want the bouncer. And you wanting him looks like you praying and actively choosing to trust God.

Anxiety is rooted in the fear of what's to come. It survives on your indulgence, your choice to embrace worst case thinking. Those first impulses to worry aren't sinful; they're simply temptations. But if those impulses aren't met with active defiance, you'll find yourself welcoming anxiety and rejecting the peace God wants to give.

The next time you read those words, "Do not be anxious about anything," don't think of them as an impossible command. See them as the generous offer they are, the promise that if you'll choose to trust God, He'll do what surpasses our understanding, protecting us with peace.

THINK & DO:

Questions to get your brain wondering...

» Paul calls the Philippians to "rejoice in the Lord always." Is that something that comes easily for you? Give an example of a time it was hard to rejoice. Were you able to? If not, what do you think you could have done differently? What does it look like to rejoice in difficult seasons? Have you ever known someone who modeled this?

» Are you known by your "gentleness" or "reasonableness" (vs 5)? Why do you think it's important for Christians to be people who listen, accept suffering and don't overreact? *Read the define section below for some helpful info on what Paul means by "gentleness."*

» Do you struggle with anxiety? What are your go-to ways of fighting it? Make a list of three things you can do when tempted to indulge in anxiety.

1.

2.

3.

» Consider Paul's list of things to think about: "whatever is true, whatever is honorable, whatever is just, whatever is pure, whatever is lovely, whatever is commendable, if there is any excellence, if there is anything worthy of praise." Make yourself a list of specific things to think about when you're tempted to let your thoughts wander into worry. Don't stop until you have twenty good and lovely things.

DEFINE:

(vs. 5) "Let your gentleness be known to all"

Some translators render this passage "reasonableness" (ESV). What it appears Paul is trying to communicate is that Christians should adopt "a humble, patient steadfastness, which is able to submit to injustice, disgrace and maltreatment without hatred or malice, trusting God in spite of it all" (R. Leivestad). This attitude endures undeserved mistreatment without throwing a fit. According to commentator P. O'Brien, "this may involve them in the patient bearing of abuse."

PRAY:

Talk to God about what's making you anxious. Make a list of your concerns and share it with Him. Ask Him to move and work in all these situations. Tell God you trust Him to take care of you no matter what.

Don't forget to thank Him, too. Thank God for all the ways you've seen Him work this week. Our thanksgiving reminds us of God's faithful presence and provision.

BECAUSE SOMETIMES LIFE STINKS

In December of 2006 my husband and I miscarried a baby. It happened in a cab on the way home from dinner in Manhattan with friends, friends sleeping on our couch for the week. They were headed to see the Christmas tree in Rockefeller Center. I begged off, had them drop me on a corner close to my subway stop. "I'll meet you at home," I said. "I'm fine," I said. And then I shut the heavy yellow door and stepped out onto the empty sidewalk. I remember it was eerily, unusually empty. I remember snow and Christmas music spilling into the street from a nearby deli. There may not have been snow, but that's how I remember it, me standing in the snow, cold, alone and keenly aware I was probably losing my baby. I walked to Starbucks, ordered a Chai tea, and tried to muster the... *I don't know*... the life? The energy? The will? It took me a half hour to get out of my chair, descend the subway stairs and catch my train.

I got home, unlocked the apartment door, climbed four flights of stairs and threw my body onto the bed like a too-heavy backpack after a long day at school. I wouldn't get up for another three days.

A week later my doctor would say in a thick Russian accent, "You'll have many babies. No problem." But there were problems, and we miscarried early again.

Looking back I feel a little guilty for being so sad—I was indefatigably sad. Now, I think of those "lost" babies and feel joy, knowing we'll meet again when I go to them. But then, then I didn't know there would be more babies. I didn't know the joy of holding an 8 pound girl, pulled from the soil of my very body, grown in me, like me. All I knew were miscarriages, babies without roots, too easily unsettled. And emptiness. I knew too well the feeling of being empty.

And then spring came. One day in March the sun came out and the temperature climbed and all of New York emerged from hibernation, stepping onto the sidewalks without coats, eyes squinting, smiles on pale faces. This day seemed too beautiful for sad, and so Justin and I took notebooks to the new park under the Brooklyn Bridge and let the sun kiss our kiss-hungry cheeks.

We talked on the way to the park, about how hard it was to believe we'd ever have a baby and how exhausting it was to be sad. We decided we didn't want to think about loss anymore. We wanted to think about good things, about lovely and excellent things. We wanted to have hope. So we prayed God would help us believe a baby was possible, and we asked for one with as much faith as we could muster.

Then, on that beautiful day in March, sitting on the grass with a couple hundred other winter-weary New Yorkers, we wrote letters to the baby we would one day have. Justin told the baby he hoped she was kind. I told the baby I hoped he was more like his dad than me.

We left the park and dropped by a baby store on the way home. We looked at cute onesies and soft blankets and instead of feeling that familiar sense of dread and despair, we felt something different, something lighter. We felt hope.

I'd find out a week or two later that we were pregnant, that we'd been pregnant even as we wrote those letters. We'd find out months later still that we'd been pregnant with our London Jane, and years later that she'd be kind and the spitting image of her mother.

I thought of this moment today among a list of other moments, times in my life when I had to make a choice: Was I going to let the difficulties drain the color from my days, anchoring me to the bed, holding me captive? Or was I going to respond to hardship with hope, believing in God's power and presence, looking for the good God was doing and would do?

My husband has a photo of our family above his desk at work. It's of the four of us dressed up in our favorite, nicest clothes, waist deep in lake water, beaming with joy. It was taken the moment after London Jane's baptism. It's my favorite picture. Beside it hangs a print with these words in gold capital letters: GOOD THINGS HAPPEN.

I see it every time I sit at that desk to help with a project or print an email or counsel a couple, and I think of Jennifer and Justin sitting under the Brooklyn Bridge choosing to believe good things happen.

They were so right.

ten

THROUGH HIM

"I have learned the secret of being content in any and every situation, whether well fed or hungry, whether living in plenty or in want. I can do all this through him who gives me strength."

READ:

Today is your LAST DAY in Philippians! Read chapter 4 verses 10-23. Look closely at the text. Try to see something you haven't seen before.

FOCUS:

"I have learned the secret." Normally that would be a super-exciting beginning to a sentence. We love secrets.

I have learned the secret to weight loss!

I have learned the secret to a clean house!

I have learned the secret to making people like me!

I have learned the secret to good sex!

This is the stuff of pop-up ad magic.

But Paul keeps talking and this secret he's learned suddenly doesn't seem so exciting, because it's the secret to, drum roll... contentment. Contentment is not sexy. Contentment says boring, tweedy things like "enough" and "I can wait" and "either way."

Contentment says, "I'm sick and not getting better. I can live with that." It says, "The money is tight. I can deal with that." It says, "All I want is a husband but I don't have one and that's just fine with me." "We want a baby, and we're asking God for one, but we're okay if He says no."

Contentment says, "What's happening around me doesn't change what's true inside me."

It's not sexy, but it may well be the most valuable thing you don't yet have. A content person can't be disrupted. A content person can't be swayed. You can't hurt the contented by taking something away. A content person always has access to joy and peace. A content person survives. No matter what.

Paul's offering the secret to contentment. Are you interested?

Before we reveal it, let's first check to see if you need it. To diagnose your resting level of contentment try filling in this blank: I couldn't live without _____. The higher the number of things you could put in that blank, the lower your level of contentment.

Now, the secret: the secret to contentment is strength from God. It's Philippians 4:13, oft-quoted and rarely understood. The ability to do all things, to survive all things, to bear up under all things is God, God who freely gives His children strength.

You need that kind of strength, the kind of strength that makes hard things doable, the kind of strength that makes impossible burdens bearable, the kind of strength that lifts eyes above physical circumstances and opens eyes to a more-real world not-so-far away.

Go wants to give you strength not so you'll be capable of doing amazing, important, fame-bringing things like winning a World Series or an Oscar or The Voice. He gives you strength so you can deal with loss, disappointment, suffering, pain, a broken leg that won't heal that means you'll never achieve your dream of winning the World Series, two hundred failed auditions for bit parts, or a tumor on your vocal chords. He gives you strength to control the voracious hunger for more than inevitably comes from winning the World Series or an Oscar or the Voice. The strength in Philippians 4:13 is strength to be content no matter what—content when the world is caving in and the burdens are stacking to the sky and opposition mounts and you think you can't keep going. And content when your blessings overflow your cup and everything seems possible and you want so much to reach for more and more and more. It's not the strength to avoid pain or even to get past it. It's the strength to keep enduring it. It's not the strength to climb the mountain of blessing and achievement even higher. It's the strength to be happy with wherever you are on the mountain.

Paul says, I'm satisfied with what I have and with what I don't have. That may be one of the hardest things for a human being to say. Fortunately, God will help us say it and mean it.

THINK & DO:

Don't skip the questions today. Sit right down and think about what you're reading...

» Have you learned to be content whatever the circumstances? If so, do you have any practices or habits that facilitate contentment? If not, how could you set yourself up for contentment success? Think of a time you were especially discontent. What was the problem?

» Does the context for Philippians 4:13 change your understanding of it? What is it that God promises to empower you to do? Where do you currently need some Phil. 4:13 strength?

» How might you share in someone's troubles (vs 14)? Do you know anyone going through a difficult time who would benefit from your support (financial or emotional)? Make a plan to be a partner.

» What is the main thing you've learned in your study of Philippians? What do you think God wants you to DO in response to your time in this book?

DEFINE:

(vs. 17) "Not that I desire your gifts; what I desire is that more be credited to your account."

Paul is acknowledging the gift sent from the Philippians via Epaphroditus. Paul very much needed the (likely financial) gift but says that more than he wants help he wants "more to be credited to your account." Paul here is stating explicitly that what matters isn't what happens on earth but what happens in Heaven. The gift the Philippians give on earth is a deposit into a Heavenly bank account; they're storing up treasure where it lasts. What that treasure is exactly isn't clear, though perhaps it's simply evidence of the Philippians' saving faith.

(vs. 19) "God will meet all your needs according to the riches of his glory in Christ Jesus."

Commentator Peter O'Brien says of this verse, "By stating that God will supply the Philippians' every need, the apostle not only echoes the preceding context and refers to their material needs, but also and more significantly he focuses on the central concerns of the letter, namely the fulfilling of their spiritual needs." There's good evidence to suggest this passage is more prayer than assertion, that what Paul's saying is more like "May God meet all your needs..." Either way, prayer or assertion, Paul believes God will do it.

PRAY:

God wants to meet all your needs—especially your spiritual needs. So what are they?

What spiritual work do you need God to do in your heart?

What spiritual power do you need?

What spiritual hungers do you have?

Look back over the course of this study and identify any spots where you felt especially needy for God's work.

Take a minute and do some beseeching. Ask God to give you what you most need.

REMEMBER BEIJING?

My husband and I watch *The Blacklist*. It's this show about a confidential informant for the FBI. He's complicated (of course), pompous, arrogant, and self-indulgent. Every episode he'll be talking to an associate of his and launch into a seemingly irrelevant story set in some exotic location. He'll lean in, narrow his eyes and say, nostalgia dripping from his words, "Remember Morocco?"

One night while we were watching, Justin paused the show, turned to me and asked, "Why don't we do that? We've been to some cool places. Why don't we ever say, 'Remember Rome?' Or London? And why don't you get angry and throw a glass of water at me and say 'Oh, I remember Rome. I'll never forget!'"

He's funny.

I liked the idea. So a few days later I sent him a text:

"Remember Beijing? That time in the forbidden city when we got separated in the emperor's quarters and, looking all over for you, I stumbled upon this exquisite, perfectly manicured garden, frosted in whiter than white snow? And there you were. A perfect thing among perfect things."

Sappy, I know, but he loved it.

I was thinking of this the other day driving home from a speaking engagement. I'd been talking about the war between spirit and flesh, how one day the fog would lift and we'd all see clearly and realize so much of what we thought was important wasn't important at all and so many other things we'd put off or put aside were the things that really, really mattered. I said, "We think of being a Christian as this tame, small thing, but really it's epic and dramatic. It's *The Hunger Games* and *Lord Of The Rings* and *Blacklist*—good versus evil in a global, celestial showdown to the death. *To the life."*

I thought, why don't we Christians begin sentences like Raymond Reddington does on *Blacklist*? And so I sent a different sort of text to Justin:

"Remember Wuhan? When we stood beside a gymnasium swimming pool in full winter dress—coat, hat, scarf—steam fogging the windows, us pretending we were there to tour the facility when really we were spies under the gaze of an oppressive Chinese government, watching our soon-to-be-brother, celebrating in packed silence the victory in the water, the whole of Heaven erupting in raucous joy."

I delighted in remembering that story of undercover, defiant faith. My hands shook as I typed it and tears fell onto the glowing screen.

I have so many of these epic memories. Every child of God and warrior of light will. Not all of them take place in exotic locations but so many are full of drama and victory and gravity. I can be tempted to forget that. Tempted to fall into the quicksand of small living. And tempted to doubt God's ability or willingness to empower adventure and risk, hamstringing my future with Christ. Everything we've learned in the book of Philippians propels us into a live or die way of seeing and being, but that kind of life takes courage and counter-cultural contentment and a whole lot of trust. I've learned over the years that courage, contentment and trust leak, that we have to keep filling the bucket with proof, reminders that God is worthy of whole-life devotion.

If we want to be people who're fully living for Christ and ever dying to self, we need to remember why it's worth the risk. Remembering (and the praise and thanksgiving that come alongside) enable perseverance. Like weary soldiers huddled around the campfire, we tell ourselves stories and sing songs, stories of God showing up, stories of victory over evil, songs of deliverance and joy, songs fueling life-charting hope.

What are the stories you tell around the fire? What are the songs you sing in the trenches, bombs going off around you, the enemy so close you can smell his cigarette?

These are the stories I tell and the songs I sing...

To my husband I say, "Remember Henderson? When we stood apart across the kitchen island, so angry and so hungry to forgive and, by the power of God, began a practice of forgiveness giving life, enabling love and joy even now?"

With my friend Janine I recall, "Remember Chick-fil-A? When we sat in a booth while our kids played on a dirty, crowded playground, and we sorted the messiness of life and realized the power of daily bread?"

With my mother I reflect, "Remember the couch? Where we sat for three hours and I listened and you did, too, and things that had seemed so hard to say suddenly weren't and we prayed and we welcomed the Spirit of God and His good work of translation and reconciliation?"

To my church, "Remember the snow? When just for a moment something impossible was possible and we remembered nothing is impossible with God?"

To my children, "Remember Hurricane Ridge? When we stood on the very top tip of a mountain surrounded by mountains and praised the God who'd made it all?"

And then there are the stories I share with God...

"God, remember Pinellas Park? Where I made tracts about salvation on the copy machine at seven years old? Where You found me and loved me and washed me clean and new?"

Remember Weeki Wachee? When I swam beside a manatee

alone underwater, the whole world quiet, You saying "It is good" and me in full, joyful agreement?

Remember Brooklyn? Where I lost a baby and found my voice? Where you held me in bed while I cried and later whispered words in my ear as I talked to friends who needed You and saw You in me?

Remember Split, on the Croatian coast? Where You filled a tiny room with Your loud, sure, joyful voice, standing in and beside and around Your people, all of us worshipping You, all of us seeing You in one another?

The remembers go on and on...

Join me, friends, in remembering. Not just in our heads but with our hearts and in our words. Let's inspire one another to more. Let's fill each other's leaky buckets with courage and contentment and trust. Let's lean across the table and say with a twinkle in our eyes and treble in our tone, "Remember..."

And then, those stories and songs still thick in the air and hot on our lips, let's rise to live. Or die.

The grace of the Lord

Jesus Christ be with your spirit.

Amen.

About the Author

Jennifer (JL) Gerhardt is a writer and storytelling minister from Round Rock, TX. Her previous books include Prayer, In Practice, Think Good *and a prayer journal for kids. She also blogs at godscout. com. As a storytelling minister for Round Rock Church of Christ she enables God's people to share their stories of redemption, rescue, and belonging in Christ.*

Jennifer is married to Justin Gerhardt, a preacher, and together they have two daughters, London (9) and Eve (8). Jennifer is an INFJ, lover of chai tea lattes, recreational swimmer, believer in the power of white paint and Dietrich Bonhoeffer fangirl.

To keep up with JL Gerhardt, subscribe to her newsletter at godscout.com/subscribe

Struggle with anxiety? Fear? Guilt? Depression?

THINK GOOD can help.

Honest, practical, personal and remarkably relatable, *Think Good* is the book to help you fix your thoughts. *Think Good* is both a better way to think and a better what to think—a mindset and mind skill enabled only by the power of our peace-giving God.

"Think Good is a profound, well-written, extremely practical resource for anyone who has ever wished they could corral their pesky thoughts and make them behave. Gerhardt references modern science, psychology, Scripture and personal experience as she debunks popular myths about our thoughts and provides a fresh new perspective on how to "think good." As someone whose brain is constantly stuck in overdrive, this book is a lifeline for me."

— Bethany W.

"There is no hocus pocus in this book, only practical advice, loving words, and exercises to point your mind to thinking good. Fear paralyzed me after tragically losing my brother in law and watching my sister become a widow and single mom last year. This book has and continues to give me the tools I need to break free from this fear and think good. It is a book that I will reread for encouragement and wisdom throughout this battle."

— Lizbeth W.

Available through all major online booksellers.

Made in the USA
Las Vegas, NV
07 February 2021